JOHN JAY

DIPLOMAT OF THE AMERICAN EXPERIMENT

JOHN JAY

DIPLOMAT OF THE AMERICAN EXPERIMENT

Casey White

rosen
central™

The Rosen Publishing Group, Inc., New York

Published in 2006 by The Rosen Publishing Group, Inc.
29 East 21st Street, New York, NY 10010

First Edition

Library of Congress Cataloging-in-Publication Data

White, Casey.
John Jay: diplomat of the american experiment/Casey White.
     p. cm.–(The library of American thinkers)
Includes bibliographical references and index.
ISBN 1-4042-0507-1 (library binding)
1. Jay, John, 1745–1829–Juvenile literature. 2. Statesmen–United States–Biography–
Juvenile literature. 3. United States–Politics and government–1775–1783–Juvenile
literature. 4. United States–Politics and government–1783–1809–Juvenile literature.
5. Judges–United States–Biography–Juvenile literature. 6. Judges–New York (State)–
Biography–Juvenile literature. 7. New York (State)–Politics and government–To
1775–Juvenile literature. I. Title. II. Series.
E302.6.J4W49 2006
973.3'092–dc22

                                                                                    2005011509

Printed in China

On the cover: Background: *Southeast Prospect of the City of New York*, circa 1756 to 1757, eighteenth century, artist unknown. Inset: John Jay, first chief justice of the Supreme Court of the United States. Oil painting by Gilbert Stuart, 1794.

CONTENTS

YA
921
J33w

           INTRODUCTION 6

Chapter 1 A VERY PLEASING PROSPECT 18

Chapter 2 "WE WILL NEVER SUBMIT" 34

Chapter 3 THE DIPLOMAT 55

Chapter 4 THE FEDERALIST 71

Chapter 5 THE MOST HATED MAN IN
               AMERICA 86

           TIMELINE 99

           GLOSSARY 102

           FOR MORE INFORMATION 105

           FOR FURTHER READING 106

           BIBLIOGRAPHY 107

           INDEX 109

INTRODUCTION

"The Americans are the first people whom Heaven has favored with an opportunity of deliberating upon and choosing the forms of government under which they should live." –John Jay

J ohn Jay is often referred to today as the "forgotten" Founding Father. It is a somewhat unflattering way to be remembered. Yet being remembered this way, even as the subject of an oxymoron, is no doubt better than being forgotten altogether. And for us, who are now responsible for the remembering, it is better that he not be forgotten. Indeed, no true understanding of the origins of this country is possible without considering Jay's contributions.

The names of the other Founding Fathers roll easily off the tongue, even for those with no particular expertise in American history: George Washington,

John Jay sat for this painting by artist Joseph Wright of Derby in 1786. This was during the time after the war when the first thirteen states of the United States were trying to form a viable government. "What astonishing changes a few years are capable of producing!" George Washington wrote to Jay from Mount Vernon in a letter on August 15 of that year.

Alexander Hamilton, John Adams, Thomas Jefferson, Benjamin Franklin, James Madison. No one questions their credentials. But John Jay? Even those who say they recognize the name probably follow that statement with a somewhat embarrassed question or two: Who was he again, exactly? What did he do again?

But the men mentioned in the previous paragraph, those better-remembered Founding Fathers, would never have questioned Jay's status or that he deserved to be numbered among them. They most likely would be surprised, if not shocked, that Jay's reputation has not better stood the test of time. Each of them, in one way or another, at one time or another, regarded Jay as "indispensable" (a word often used to describe Jay in his lifetime).

A list of his various titles and achievements would seem to be enough to ensure Jay's reputation for posterity: delegate to the Continental Congress, primary author of the New York Constitution, president of the Continental Congress, foreign minister to Spain, peace commissioner to France, author of *The Federalist*, first chief justice of the U.S. Supreme Court, special envoy to England, valued adviser to the president of the United States, and governor of New York.

So why is Jay's life, with his many achievements, not more widely known and celebrated today? In part, it might be because his accomplishments were so numerous and diverse. Although it hardly does them justice, it is relatively easy to

Benjamin Franklin was the most famous American at the time leading up to the American Revolution. He was also one of the most radical members of the Continental Congress, often criticizing the boldest of proposed measures against England as still not going far enough.

sum up the life and achievements of the other Founding Fathers in a few words or a short phrase. George Washington? The father of his country; first president. Thomas Jefferson? Author of the Declaration of Independence. James Madison? Architect of the Constitution. Alexander Hamilton? First secretary of the treasury; engineer of the American economy. John Adams? The Sage of Braintree (Braintree was Adams's hometown in Massachusetts). Benjamin Franklin? Old Lightning Rod, as both his many supporters and enemies called him. And so on.

George Washington could have easily assumed power equal to that of Napoléon or Julius Caesar if he had wanted to do so. There were even supporters of this idea. His feelings about this are evident in a letter he wrote to Jay in 1786. "I am told that even respectable characters speak of a monarchical form of government without horror. From thinking proceeds speaking, thence to acting is often but a single step. But how irrevocable & tremendous!"

Jay's career is much harder to sum up neatly. He was not a war hero like Washington, a leader of the Continental Congress like Adams, or a force at the Constitutional Convention like Madison. He was not a dazzlingly brilliant man of many interests like Jefferson, Franklin, or Hamilton. He is probably most often remembered as the first chief justice of the U.S. Supreme Court, but his tenure there was actually brief and undistinguished. The people of the United States during his lifetime would most likely have immediately identified Jay with the 1794 agreement with Great Britain generally referred to, mostly derisively, as the Jay Treaty. It was Jay's misfortune that the one thing for which he received full credit also represented the low point of his career.

Jay lacked, for example, the simple physical presence, the assumed air of dignity and command, with which Washington seemed to overawe his compatriots. He had none of the dash and studied, democratic, disheveled elegance of Jefferson. Nor did he exude Jefferson's immediate, casual, offhand brilliance. He did not possess the polymath's mastery of a seeming infinity of subject matter, as did Jefferson and Franklin. Although he was a skillful writer, his words seldom inspired and provoked in the ways of Patrick Henry's or Jefferson's or Hamilton's. Moreover, he was not a tireless, inextinguishable, volcanic torrent of ideas, opinions, quarrels, and criticisms like the temperamental Adams. A courteous host and a polite guest, he did not sparkle in conversation and shine in company like the voluble Franklin and the handsome, charming Hamilton; a book of the witty sayings of John Jay would be a short volume indeed. For better or worse, his life lacked much of the drama that characterized Jefferson's and Hamilton's, with their illicit, scandalous love affairs and romantic liaisons, their bitter feuds that encompassed both personal and political passions. There was certainly nothing in Jay's life to compare with Hamilton's tragic vendetta against Aaron Burr, which led to the singular consequence of the first secretary of the treasury being shot to death by the former vice president of the United States.

Perhaps here we have the reason for Jay's relative anonymity today: his personality. He was reliable rather than inspirational, solid and admirable without rising to the heroic. He somehow lacked the color, the flair, that indefinable essence known as charisma that the other Founding Fathers possessed in such abundance. Almost always, he was a moderate man defending radical propositions. He was an unlikely revolutionary. His watchwords were reason, patience, caution, good counsel, integrity, and diplomacy. He was initially slow to embrace the cause of American independence and maintained to the end of his life that the American Revolution occurred only because the British forced the colonists into it. For Jay, the American Revolution was never a sacred cause of liberty and a strike against monarchy, as it was for Jefferson and his partisans. For Jay, the revolution was something more practical than idealistic. Moreover, he distrusted democracy, regarding it as a necessary but flawed system and believing that the power of the vote should be as limited as possible. No one would deny that John Jay was a patriot, but he made an unlikely rebel.

But if Jay is thus fated to seem a somewhat drab figure next to his more colorful contemporaries, one needs to acknowledge that Jay's personality also served him remarkably well. Indeed, it was his personality and character that made him, in the estimate of the other Founding Fathers, so essential, so indispensable. Often forgotten is how fractious the relationships between the founders could be. This was particularly true

John Adams was the first vice president of the United States and the second president, defeating Thomas Jefferson. Adams and Jefferson were rivals but initially had been friends. Both men died on July 4, 1826. Upon his deathbed, Adams muttered, "At least Jefferson survives." However, Jefferson had died just a few hours earlier.

during the presidencies of Washington and Adams. At that point the unity bred by the shared causes of the Revolution and the Constitution was behind them. The focus had turned to the day-to-day work of establishing a functioning government and using it to build a viable, independent nation.

By that time, the Founding Fathers were not always mutual admirers. Franklin, by far the oldest of them, was dead. His followers and admirers, led by his grandson, the publisher of an influential Philadelphia newspaper, carried on with unrelenting criticism of first the revered Washington and then

Thomas Jefferson, like Benjamin Franklin, was a man of numerous roles, not excluding architect and founder of the University of Virginia. As the third president of the United States, he famously made the Louisiana Purchase and dispatched the Lewis and Clark expedition.

Adams. They also had little use for Hamilton. The more devoted of these critics asserted that it was Franklin, rather than Washington, who truly deserved to be known as the father of his country. Though members of the same party, Hamilton and Adams came to hate each other almost as much as Adams and Franklin had. Jefferson and Hamilton despised one another, personally and politically, as did Jefferson and Adams in the postrevolutionary period before a reconciliation late in life. As Jefferson's closest confidante, Madison largely shared his alliances and enmities. Madison and Hamilton

Alexander Hamilton was born in the Caribbean. He was abandoned by his father, and his mother died when he was a teenager. He gained the opportunity to go to New York to study through the support and generosity of benefactors. He met John Jay soon after his arrival. Jay helped Hamilton become established in New York.

were at one time close friends, collaborators in planning the Constitution, but they fell out as the rivalry between Jefferson and Hamilton intensified. Washington, who was exceptionally close to Hamilton, strove to remain above the fray but was deeply wounded by the criticisms leveled by Franklin's and Jefferson's supporters. His relationship with Jefferson suffered as a result. Though Washington and Adams respected each other, they did not get along particularly well.

Jay, however, managed to earn and keep the friendship, trust, and respect of all these men. This was an admirable feat

James Madison sought to limit the power of the federal government as a member of Congress after the Constitution was ratified. Jefferson and Madison's opposition to a national bank led to the creation of the first political parties in the United States. He was the fourth president of the United States, and at 5'4" (163 cm) and 100 pounds (45 kg), was also the smallest.

among such powerful personalities in such tumultuous times. He was a skilled diplomat, in both personal relationships and relations between nations. This made him a most valuable individual in the most critical of times—an indispensable man for most situations. The words of Jay's initial charge to the grand jury, at the opening of his term as chief justice of the Supreme Court, well reflect his philosophy toward the great American experiment: "Let it be remembered that civil liberty consists, not in a right to every man to do just what he pleases, but it consists in an equal right to all citizens to have, enjoy, and do, in peace, security, and without molestation, whatever the equal and constitutional laws of the country admit to be consistent with the public good." It is a moderate stating of a radical proposition; at the time America's experiment with liberty and self-government under a written constitution was a radical idea, something that had never been successfully tried before.

Jay's greatness was that despite his instinctive moderation and caution, he nonetheless recognized the beauty and value, in terms of human progress and liberty, that this radical American experiment represented.

CHAPTER
1

A VERY PLEASING PROSPECT

A nother way in which Jay differed from the other Founding Fathers was in his ancestry. For Adams, Washington, Franklin, Jefferson, Madison, and Hamilton, England truly was the mother country. All these men were of English ancestry, as were the majority of Americans at that time. (Hamilton was half-Scottish.)

Jay, however, was of French and Dutch ancestry. He was born in New York City on December 12, 1745, probably in the house his father owned at 66 Pearl Street in what is now lower Manhattan. He was baptized several days later at Trinity Church, also in lower Manhattan. Trinity was an Episcopal church. Jay would

This 1780 map depicts parts of Connecticut, as well as Long Island, and New York and Westchester counties. John Jay grew up in Rye, located on the Long Island Sound, just below the southernmost tip of the boundary of Fairfield County in Connecticut on this map. Rye was a typical American town at the time, with a small central downtown where an inn and a couple of churches were located, surrounded by various farms and farmhouses.

remain a regular churchgoer and believer in Christian teachings for the rest of his life. This was another way in which he differed from Washington, Franklin, and Jefferson, all of whom were skeptics in one way or another about organized religion and Christian doctrine.

New York had begun as a Dutch possession. That made it unique among the thirteen colonies, as did the national and ethnic diversity of its settlers. By the mid-1600s, eighteen

This painting, titled *Southeast Prospect of New York*, is a view of the city of New York, circa 1756 to 1757. Almost from its beginnings, New York was known as a cosmopolitan, ethnically diverse city. It was a colony based on commerce (the basis of its economic power is evident here) rather than religion. After the British took it from the Dutch, it became Britain's military headquarters in the New World.

different languages were commonly spoken in New Amsterdam, as both the colony and its chief city were known. By that time, the city of New Amsterdam was already showing signs of becoming one of North America's most important trading and commercial centers and ports.

New Amsterdam

As a Dutch bastion surrounded by English colonies, New Amsterdam was always in a precarious position regarding its survival as a Dutch possession. England had claimed it at virtually the same time as the Netherlands. As New Amsterdam steadily grew, England continued to covet it. The Hudson River had immediately been recognized as an important waterway, potentially even more so for the English than for the Dutch. It offered a potential connection by water to the rich fur-trading lands claimed by the British to the north in Canada. The land on both sides of the Hudson, which runs southward and divided the region in two, was rich farmland, and New Amsterdam seemed obviously destined to become an economic hub of the New World.

Accordingly, in 1664, England sent troops to wrest New Amsterdam away from the Dutch. Preoccupied with fighting in Europe and securing its overseas holdings in the Spice Islands of the East Indies (present-day Indonesia and the Banda Islands), the Netherlands did not send forces to the colony's aid. Peter Stuyvesant, the Dutch governor of New Amsterdam, tried to rally the colonists to resist the British, only to find them indifferent, if not downright enthusiastic, about the potential change in colonial masters. Stuyvesant himself was an unlovable, tyrannical leader, and even under his predecessors the New Amsterdam colonists had enjoyed much fewer rights to self-government than did their neighbors in the British colonies. The colonists of New Amsterdam were not able to elect their own colonial legislatures, for example, as was the practice in the English colonies. The colonists of New Amsterdam had also embraced its obvious commercial potential. The merchants and traders of the city of New Amsterdam were particularly enthusiastic about the change in rule because they thought it would bring increased trade with the rich English colonies. Stuyvesant was thus forced to surrender New Amsterdam to the English without resistance. The English named their new possession New York.

Peter Stuyvesant lost his leg in a battle with Spanish forces three years before arriving in New Amsterdam from the Caribbean. He was sent there to bring order to the wild and unruly settlement. He soon implemented strict rules such as mandatory church attendance and the fencing in of all large animals. Stuyvesant is credited as the first person to introduce tea to North America.

THE JAYS IN NEW YORK

Jay's upbringing reflected this history. His ancestors were Dutch and French rather than English. His father, Peter Jay, was born in New York City in 1704. Both Peter's father, Auguste, and grandfather, Pierre, were Huguenots, as Protestants in France were known. Both were driven from France in the seventeenth century, with Pierre finding refuge in England and Auguste fleeing directly to the New World, first to South Carolina and then Philadelphia before settling in New York City. The Jays felt great resentment toward France for the way they and their coreligionists had been treated, and tremendous

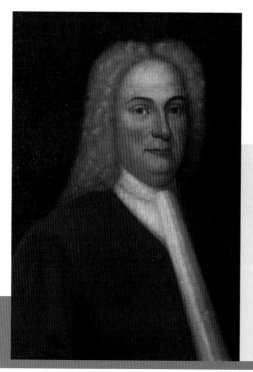

John Jay's grandfather Auguste Jay established the Jays in New York after escaping France, following the revocation of the Edict of the Nantes by Louis XIV in 1685. The Edict of Nantes had been instituted by King Henry IV of France in 1598 to grant French Protestants civil rights. This revocation caused about half a million skilled artisans and intellectuals to leave France, often taking up the cause of Protestant-friendly countries against France afterward.

gratitude toward England for giving Pierre a safe haven. It was a tradition that John Jay continued; in his diplomatic career he was always more amenable toward England than to France.

Auguste Jay was quick to seize the opportunities the New World offered. In New York, he changed his first name to the more English-sounding Augustus and soon found work as a supercargo aboard trading ships owned by Frederick Philipse, the richest man in the New York colony. A supercargo was an officer on a trading ship with the overall responsibility for the business and commercial concerns of the voyage. It was a very important position on the ship. It was as important, if not more so in some ways, as the captain's position.

Philipse's trade was primarily with Madagascar, a large island in the Indian Ocean off the east coast of Africa. For the outward voyage, Auguste Jay would make sure Philipse's ships were laden with rum, wine, beer, tobacco, and fabric and clothing. At Madagascar and nearby islands, those goods would be exchanged for furniture, spices, and the most lucrative "goods" of all, African slaves. It made Philipse an immensely wealthy man. Auguste Jay was soon doing very well for himself also, financially and socially. His business success enabled him to marry a woman of Dutch ancestry who was related to the most prominent and important remaining Dutch families in the city of New York, such as the Van Cortlandts and the Stuyvesants.

Their son, Peter, learned about the perils, pitfalls, and profits of overseas trading from his father. He became an extremely successful merchant in his own right, shipping American timber, furs, and grain from New York to England, Ireland, and Holland in exchange for cloth, clothing, and flaxseed. The woman he married, John Jay's mother, Mary, was both a Van Cortlandt and a Philipse.

JAY'S CHILDHOOD IN RYE, NEW YORK

John Jay's family was thus both wealthy and extremely prominent socially. By 1745, the year of John's birth, Peter Jay was comfortable enough to have retired from trading. That year, he also moved his family from New York City to a

400-acre (162-hectare) farm near the town of Rye in Westchester County, about twenty miles (thirty-two kilometers) northeast of New York City on Long Island Sound, not far from the colony's border with Connecticut. This was where John Jay spent most of his childhood. The farm seems to have been more a wealthy gentleman's country retreat than a viable agricultural concern, although Peter did keep several slaves to help with the work there.

John was the sixth of seven surviving children, five boys and two girls. In some ways, though, he was treated as a first or only son. Of his five older siblings, two were mentally ill, and two more had been blinded by smallpox at a young age. James, the only healthy older sibling, left home when John was four to study medicine in Edinburgh, Scotland; their relationship was always distant and ultimately turned hostile (James became a Loyalist during the American Revolution and was knighted in England).

GREAT EXPECTATIONS

Jay's father had high hopes for him from a young age. Schooled first at home, Jay by the age of six was already exhibiting signs of the personality and abilities that would characterize him. These signs led his father to praise, in a letter to relatives at that time, his young son's precocious ability at Latin and his "grave disposition." A year later, in a letter to a cousin,

Much of what is known today about Peter Jay, John Jay's father, comes from his correspondence with cousins in Paris and La Rochelle, France, and those who resided in Bristol, England, as well as letters to his sons John and James. He was a serious, severe gentleman, yet one letter from his cousin David in Bristol revealed a lighter side of Peter: David wanted a report on the charming and beautiful American girls that Peter had told him about.

Peter was even more effusive about little John's gifts, writing, "my Johnny also gives me a very pleasing prospect. He seems to be endowed with a very good capacity, is very reserved and quite of his brother James's disposition for books. He has made a beginning at the Latin and gives reason to expect that he will succeed very well."

To further those expectations, Jay was sent, at about the age of eight, to live and study at a private boarding school in New Rochelle, a town founded by Huguenots about 8 miles (13 km) southwest of Rye. Although the school had an excellent reputation, it is uncertain how much it did to develop Jay's intellectual abilities. Years later, his own son William, in a biography of his famous father, portrayed the schoolmaster there as a silly, stingy, absent-minded crackpot, so neglectful of his students that on winter nights, snow drifted in onto John's bedspread through broken windowpanes. Whether this account is exaggerated or not, by the age of ten John was back at the family farm in Rye, being taught by a private tutor.

Jay's College Days

Apparently this method of education proved more effective, for in the fall of 1760, at the age of fourteen, Jay left home for good to enroll in King's College in New York City. Eventually, King's College would become New York's famous Columbia University, but at the time it was a new, much smaller, much less prestigious institution. At the time of Jay's enrollment, King's College was just six years old, and there were just six students in Jay's incoming class. That number would diminish as Jay proceeded through the years of his college education; he and another classmate were the only members of his graduating class in 1764.

At King's College, Jay received what was then the standard education for a young gentleman who was considering entering a profession. His first years included "refresher" courses in Greek and Latin (students were assumed to have mastered those languages before enrolling, but it was also assumed they would benefit from some review work) as well as the standard courses in rhetoric (persuasive writing and speaking), oratory (public speaking), and logic. Perhaps reflecting his somewhat introspective personality, Jay initially had trouble with oratory: his teachers found that he did articulate well, but he could not pronounce the letter "l" correctly. This sometimes made him the butt of ridicule and mockery. To compensate, he purchased his own book on oratory and studied and practiced alone in his room daily. He greatly improved, but Jay would never be known as a scintillating public speaker.

In his second year at the college, Jay continued to study Greek and Latin, which were supplemented by courses in English, classics (Greek and Latin literature), mathematics, and science. In his third year, Jay and his fellow students took more classics along with what was then called natural philosophy. Today, the course would be considered essentially physical sciences, as it encompassed optics, chemistry, mechanics, and astronomy. This was Jay's least favorite course. His fourth and final year was spent in intensive study of the works of the ancient Greek historians Thucydides and Herodotus. Knowledge of these works was considered essential not just to a complete education but for any young man contemplating playing a role in the public life of his community. By that time Jay had also decided to take up law as a profession, so he studied the work of Hugo Grotius, the early seventeenth-century Dutch scholar whose thought was then considered to be the foundation of European international law.

JAY'S PHYSICALITY AND CHARACTER

John Jay graduated from King's College on May 22, 1764. He was eighteen years old and now ready to go out in the world. Tall for a man of that time at almost 6 feet (1.8 meters) in height, he was also extremely thin, even gaunt, with a very pale complexion. These characteristics would distinguish him throughout the rest of his life. His single most arresting physical feature was his piercing blue-gray eyes. The personality he would show to the world for years to come was already much in evidence. He described himself, in a letter to his best friend, Robert Livingston, as being a mixture of "bashfulness," pride, ambition, and "unbounded confidence." His father characterized him as a "youth remarkably sedate," while others described him, as acquaintances would throughout his life, as being either severe, reserved, or quiet, though usually agreeable, courteous, and polite. Some found that his pride

Hugo Grotius is considered the father of international law. His philosophy was that all laws should be divided into what is the will of God and what is of reason. He believed the only justification for war was to protect or obtain a right. "For justice brings peace of conscience, while injustice brings torment and anguish . . . Justice is approved, and injustice condemned, by the common agreement of men," Grotius wrote in *Prolegomena to the Law of War and Peace* in 1625.

sometimes made him appear pompous. Though usually even-keeled, he was prone to occasional flashes of temper. A regular churchgoer, he confessed to enjoying few pleasures and to possessing a poor understanding of the motivations and behavior of other people.

He could also be maddeningly stubborn, particularly on what he regarded as points of integrity. A few months before his graduation, for example, some rowdy students vandalized the King's College dining hall. The president of the college interrogated all who had been present. Jay's fellow students all denied both responsibility for the incident and any knowledge of who was involved. When Jay was questioned, however, he told the president that he knew who was responsible but would not reveal their names; he apparently regarded it as a point of pride to neither lie about his knowledge of the incident nor "fink" on his fellow students.

His stubborn integrity earned him a suspension of several weeks that for a time threatened his graduation and future prospects, but the college eventually relented and reinstated him in time for him to graduate with honors. If his family's wealth and social prominence were not enough, his graduation from a college further marked him as a young man with exceptional prospects. At the time, probably fewer than 1 in 100 men in the colonies had a college education. (Women were not admitted to colleges.) Jay left school to begin his professional career with his father's admonition in a letter to him in mind: "I hope you'll closely attend to [the law] with a firm resolution that no difficulties in prosecuting that study shall discourage you from applying very close to it, and if possible taking a delight in it."

CHAPTER 2

"WE WILL NEVER SUBMIT"

There were no law schools in the thirteen colonies in 1764. (The first university in the United States to offer professional training in the law was the College of William and Mary, in Williamsburg, Virginia, beginning in 1779.) A young man who wished to practice law had to find an established lawyer who was willing to take him on as a law clerk. The young man (or more likely his family) paid the lawyer for this privilege. After successfully completing this clerkship, the prospective lawyer had to then present evidence to the established lawyers of a jurisdiction (the bar) that he was deserving of admission to practice law as one of them. Today,

This is a view of Wall Street circa 1774 with insets of Trinity Church *(left)* and a statue of William Pitt, the British prime minister, at Bowling Green *(right)*. At this time, New York City was still concentrated on the lower tip of the island of Manhattan and had a population of 25,000. Also around this time, the city's inhabitants were starting to take sides as Patriots or Loyalists, and John Jay was on the brink of entering the political arena. Bowling Green was a public park that also included a statue of George III beside Pitt. Both monuments were very unpopular with the Patriots and were often vandalized and finally toppled. George III's statue would provide the lead for some 40,000 patriot bullets.

the primary criterion for admission to a state bar is by passing a comprehensive examination. However, in Jay's day it usually only required an established lawyer to vouch for the applicant's knowledge of the law. The young prospect was probably also asked to provide testimonials of his good name and character.

In Jay's case, his father paid for him to be taken on as a clerk by Benjamin Kissam, a prominent New York attorney.

During the colonial period, taverns were important meeting places where business was conducted, the latest gossip and news of the growing unrest with Britain was passed along, and strangers could meet and mingle. Fraunces Tavern was a meeting place of the New York Sons of Liberty, the site of General George Washington's famous farewell speech to his officers in 1783, and John Jay's Department of Foreign Affairs from 1785 to 1788. Today it is a national landmark and museum.

Robert R. Livingston Jr. was a year younger than his best friend and legal partner, John Jay. Though both were very confident men, letters reveal that Livingston was more socially graceful and charismatic. He would later serve as a member of the committee that drafted the Declaration of Independence and as an envoy to Paris to negotiate the terms of the Louisiana Purchase.

As was customary in New York at the time, Jay's term of clerkship was five years. During this time he agreed to perform the traditional duties of a law clerk, most of which consisted of the laborious work of copying legal documents by hand. It was work both time consuming and tedious, but Kissam agreed that in the last two years of his clerkship Jay would be given much more free time to "read" the law on his own. During Jay's time with Kissam, the city's lawyers changed their rules for admission, reducing the necessary time spent in a clerkship from five to three years. Jay had agreed to provide Kissam with five years of service as a clerk, but Kissam agreed to release him from his obligations after four.

In Kissam's law office, as he seemed to do at each station of his life, Jay impressed those around him with his diligence. Older men invariably liked Jay, finding in him a steadiness of character and seriousness of purpose unusual in someone his age. Kissam was no exception. Within just a few months of his beginning at the office, Peter Jay was able to report to a friend by letter that John "was very happily placed, with a gentleman who is extremely fond of him and who spares no pains in instructing of him." His fellow clerk in Kissam's office was Lindley Murray. In his 1827 *Memoirs* Murray described Jay as "remarkable for strong reasoning powers, comprehensive views, indefatigable application, and uncommon firmness of mind."

THE SUCCESSFUL YOUNG LAWYER

Not surprisingly, Jay was immediately accepted to the bar as soon as he applied, in October 1768. Along with his best friend, Robert Livingston, he was one of only two lawyers admitted to the bar that year. There were in all only thirty lawyers then licensed to practice in New York City, which was then, with a population of 18,000, the second-largest city in the colonies (next to Philadelphia). Rather than apply to join an established legal practice, Jay decided to open a law office of his own, in partnership with Livingston. He was immediately successful, in large part because of work referred to him by Kissam. He was so successful in fact, that in 1770 he dissolved

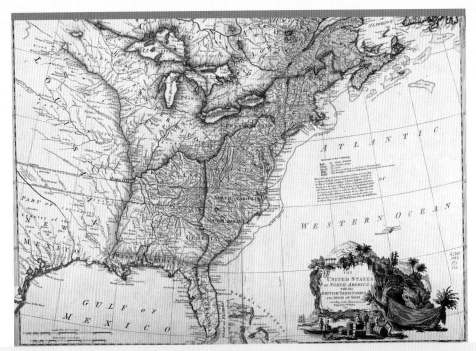

This map, titled *The United States of North America, with the British Territories*, was created in 1793. It depicts North America during the post-Revolutionary period. Colors mark the territories of various nations, including red for Great Britain and yellow for the United States. Green marks the territories for Spain, blue outlines France's Newfoundland fisheries, and Native American lands are outlined in purple and mainly encompass the Great Lakes.

his partnership with Livingston and set out on his own. (The two would, much more gradually, grow apart as friends as well: by the 1790s they were bitter political enemies.)

Like most lawyers of the day, Jay was an all-purpose practitioner, taking whatever work came to him. The majority of his practice consisted of trying to collect debts for commercial clients. He also handled criminal matters when they came his way. He worked for several years as a member of a commission

Sarah Livingston Jay was known for her love for the latest fashions. Abigail Adams Smith, daughter of John and Abigail Adams, remarked to her mother upon meeting Sarah at a dinner party that Sarah dressed "showily" but indeed was very pleasant. Although always very supportive of her husband, Sarah Jay was nonetheless glad that women were not obligated to serve in Congress, as she regarded the arguing and debating she witnessed there as unseemly and uncouth.

appointed to resolve a longstanding border dispute between New York and New Jersey.

By 1774, Jay was earning more from his practice than any other lawyer in New York. Career success brought increased social confidence, and he became a well-regarded member of a social club that met regularly at Fraunces Tavern in lower Manhattan. He even, for a little while, managed a "dancing assembly," which is where he probably met Sarah Livingston, a member of the same politically influential family as his friend Robert Livingston. Just sixteen at the time she met Jay, Sarah Livingston was described by all who knew her then as lively, beautiful, smart, and something of a flirt. Some believed Jay to be too dull for her, but Sarah thought differently, and they were married in the Livingston family home on April 28, 1774. Although events would make a quiet, domestic life impossible, their marriage would prove to be a close and happy one.

THE SEEDS OF REVOLUTION ARE PLANTED

While training for and building his career, Jay had managed to remain largely uninvolved in the defining public and political issue of the day—the increasingly contentious relationship between Great Britain and its thirteen American colonies. In 1763, Great Britain and its allies had emerged victorious from a costly war with France. Fighting in the Seven Years' War took place in North America, Europe, Asia, and on the high seas. The North American portion of the conflict was known as the French and Indian War.

Its victory allowed Great Britain to secure and even expand its vast overseas empire and wield greater power in Europe, but it came at a high price. The expenditures necessary to prosecute this worldwide conflict left Britain's finances in desperate straits. In the period afterward the British government began to seek new sources of revenue. One solution it came up with was direct taxation of its American colonies. This was a measure Britain sought to justify by citing the cost it had paid to defend the colonies against the French and their Native American allies in the recently concluded war.

The American colonists did not find Britain's argument convincing, especially as it was immediately accompanied by a measure (the Proclamation of 1763) that limited colonial settlement to the lands east of the Appalachian Mountains. For the colonies along the eastern seaboard, the natural overseas trading partner was England, via the Atlantic, and the British wanted to keep it that way. For settlements on the far side of the Appalachians, the natural trade outlet would have been the port city of New Orleans, via the Mississippi River. By terms of the peace treaty that ended the Seven Years' War, New Orleans was now a Spanish possession. Many of the colonies had already made extensive land claims across the Appalachians, and they naturally resented this new check on their opportunities for expansion.

No Taxation Without Representation

The colonists' anger rose with the imposition of Britain's first revenue measure for the colonies, the Stamp Act, in 1765. The act was a tax requiring the colonists to buy an official

The day before the Stamp Act was to go into effect, a local newspaper printed the words "death of liberty." Mobs roamed the streets, and finally 2,000 rioters gathered at Bowling Green in front of Fort George, as illustrated here. This illustration depicts the scene at Bowling Green, with the New Yorkers burning stamps.

government stamp, or license, for virtually all forms of printed material, including newspapers, pamphlets, and legal documents. The Stamp Act met with intense, sometimes violent, opposition, especially in Boston, New York, and Philadelphia, which were the centers of printing and publishing in the colonies. The colonists opposed the Stamp Act not just for the economic burden it imposed, but also because it gave

This is a nineteenth-century depiction of the House of Commons of British parliament. Today, the House of Commons is made up of more than 600 members who are directly elected. At the time of the American Revolution, voting for the House of Commons was limited to about one-fifth of the adult males in England. Besides the House of Commons, the British parliament consists of the king or queen and the unelected, hereditary body known as the House of Lords.

the British government a potential tool for controlling the distribution of published matter and with it the circulation of ideas and opinions.

The colonists also resented the act as an affront to their rights as British subjects. Practically from the time of their creation, the colonies had the right to govern themselves through elected assemblies. They regarded this right as particularly applicable to the subject of taxation. "No taxation without representation" became their rallying cry, as the colonists argued that the British parliament had no right to tax them since they did not elect representatives to that parliament. Although it made for a powerful and popular slogan, it is doubtful that the colonists would have actually wanted direct representation in Parliament, where their representatives would have been consistently and easily outvoted. At this point, the colonists still regarded themselves as British subjects. Nonetheless, they wanted the right to govern themselves through their own colonial assemblies with as little interference as possible from the British government. They regarded this as their fundamental right as British subjects.

Colonial opposition, in the form of boycotts and other means of resistance, quickly forced the British government to rescind the Stamp Act. However, it was followed two years later, in 1767, by the Townshend Acts, which imposed taxes on such essential items as glass, lead, paint, paper, and tea. Again, resistance was fierce and immediate, with the British especially disconcerted by the colonists' practice of sending circulars to all the colonies as a means of building unity, coordinating opposition, and keeping all the colonies up-to-date on developments. Initially formed in New York and Boston to resist the Stamp Act, organizations known as the Sons of Liberty now led the resistance in all thirteen colonies. The Sons of Liberty used propaganda, social pressure, and the threat of organized and mob violence to ensure compliance with the boycotts and similar measures. The so-called Committees of Correspondence made sure that letters and other communications about these events and measures were properly circulated throughout the various colonies.

A Call to Unify

Britain responded by sending troops to Boston, Massachusetts, which had emerged as the center of most direct resistance. The Bostonians hated the troops' presence, and taunting and harassment of the troops became a regular occurrence. On March 5, 1770, as a crowd was harassing British troops on the Boston Commons by throwing snowballs at them, the redcoats opened fire, killing five Bostonians and wounding several others.

The Boston Massacre, as the incident quickly became known, further inflamed colonial sentiment against the British.

Various actions and responses to the rebellion and unrest in colonial New York City are depicted in this illustration. In the foreground, a liberty pole is being raised by the New York Sons of Liberty near a recruiting booth for volunteers for the rebel cause. In the background, a tavern's sign that has an image of George III is being torn down, while Loyalists *(left foreground)* react in disgust to all of these actions against the mother country.

Again, Britain backed down, rescinding all the Townshend Acts except for the one on tea. The colonies remained solid in their boycott of British tea, however, relying largely on tea smuggled from Holland or going without. As a result, the British East India Company, which enjoyed a government monopoly on Britain's trade with the Indies, suffered severe financial damage. The company had depended on the thirteen colonies as a market for the tea it exported from India. As an

ADVERTISEMENT.

THE Members of the Affociation of the Sons of Liberty, are requefted to meet at the City-Hall, at one o'Clock, To-morrow, (being Friday) on Bufinefs of the utmoft Importance ;—And every other Friend to the Liberties, and Trade of America, are hereby moft cordially invited, to meet at the fame Time and Place.   *The Committee of the Affociation.*

Thurfday, NEW-YORK, 16th December, 1773.

This poster calls for the New York Sons of Liberty and all other supporters of the rebellion to meet at City Hall in New York. This advertisement was published on the same date that the Boston Tea Party took place. At the meeting, the protesters proclaimed that British tea ships would not be allowed to land in New York Harbor.

effort to save the company, Parliament responded with the Tea Act of 1773. This action exempted the British East India Company from all import/export duties on tea in the colonies while still requiring the colonies to pay the tea tax. Britain's idea was to thereby make its tea less expensive than that imported by the colonies from Holland. The measure only incited the most unified colonial opposition yet, with the colonists vowing not to allow any British tea to enter through their ports.

On the night of December 16, 1773, three tea-laden British East India Company ships were at anchor in Boston Harbor. Dressed as Mohawk Indians, 150 Bostonians rowed out to the vessels, boarded them, chopped open 342 tea chests with hatchets, and poured the tea into the cold, dark waters of the harbor. Circulated by the Sons of Liberty, news of the Boston Tea Party spread quickly to the other colonies, arousing great excitement and inspiring similar acts in New York, Philadelphia, and other places.

Parliament and Britain's King George III responded with what the colonists dubbed the Intolerable Acts. The colonists felt the most onerous of these measures was the closing of Boston Harbor to all shipping and the requirement to quarter (house) British troops in public inns and taverns, unoccupied buildings, and even in private homes. The colonies determined that even greater unity was required in response and decided to convene a gathering of delegates from each of the colonies to decide on a unified course of action. Thus, in September 1774, the First Continental Congress met in Philadelphia.

Jay and the First Continental Congress

Among its participants, as a member of the New York delegation, was the successful young lawyer John Jay. His selection is an indication of the stature he had achieved as a member of the New York bar. At that time he had not been part of the anti-British agitation in his colony. New York, like Boston, had been the site of rioting and other disturbances following the imposition of the Stamp Act, but Jay took no part. In fact, when opposition to the Stamp Act kept Kissam from acquiring the necessary stamps for his legal documents, Jay took advantage of this disruption of business to take a vacation in New England with his friend Robert Livingston. He leisurely read and went horseback riding. Similarly, when Britain shut down New York's colonial assembly in response to the colony's bitter opposition to the Townshend Acts, Jay was not among the many young leaders in the colony who penned articles and met to discuss other means of resistance.

It is difficult to say whether Jay participated in the First Continental Congress more as a matter of duty or conviction. He was far from being one of the best known of the delegates. That honor belonged to men like Samuel Adams, the leader of the most radical faction from Massachusetts. Or the honor went to Richard Henry Lee and Patrick Henry from Virginia, who was famous for his fiery, impassioned oratory. John Dickinson of Pennsylvania was also famous at the time of the congress for the letters he had published under the pen name "Pennsylvania Farmer," and in which he advocated resistance to Britain's revenue measures.

Although Jay was immediately grouped with the more moderate and even conservative factions at the congress, he quickly earned respect for his well-stated articulation of his

To the Public.

THE long expected TEA SHIP arrived laſt night at Sandy-Hook, but the pilot would not bring up the Captain till the ſenſe of the city was known. The committee were immediately informed of her arrival, and that the Captain ſolicits for liberty to come up to provide neceſſaries for his return. The ſhip to remain at Sandy-Hook. The committee conceiving it to be the ſenſe of the city that he ſhould have ſuch liberty, ſignified it to the Gentleman who is to ſupply him with proviſions, and other neceſſaries. Advice of this was immediately diſpatched to the Captain ; and whenever he comes up, care will be taken that he does not enter at the cuſtom-houſe, and that no time be loſt in diſpatching him.

New-York, April 19, 1774.

This announcement distributed by the New York Sons of Liberty warns of a tea ship landing in New York Harbor. Thus, the New York tea party took place in late April 1774, just a short time after the famous Boston Tea Party (December 16, 1773). John Jay and Sarah Livingston were not in New York City at the time. They were in Elizabethtown, New York, preparing for their wedding.

view that it was premature for the colonies to be thinking about going to war with Britain. This put him at odds with firebrands such as Lee and Henry, who wished to raise and arm colonial militias immediately. Yet it reflected what was the majority opinion of the congress at that time. Jay argued that the colonies basically had three alternatives: negotiation with Britain, an even more stringent trade boycott, or war. He was, as John Adams's notes confirm, in favor of negotiation and boycott as the next steps to be taken.

It is clear, however, that Jay hoped ultimately for a reconciliation with England rather than a permanent break. In a letter written to a friend in England at the time, he said, "God knows how the contest will end. I sincerely wish it may terminate in a lasting union with Great Britain."

When the congress decided to draft an address to the people of Great Britain explaining the American position, Jay was one of the three men chosen, along with Lee and Robert Livingston, to draw up drafts. It was Jay's draft of the address that was adopted by the congress and that so impressed Jefferson. In "The Address to the People of Great Britain," Jay sought to assure the British people that the Americans were not rebellious, ungovernable, and determined on independence. He cited the ways in which Britain's imposition of its various revenue acts and its treatment of the city of Boston following the Boston Tea Party violated the colonists' rights. He informed the British that all the Americans wanted was to be "free as yourselves." If Parliament and the Crown could see the justice in this, he wrote, then the colonists would be happy to forever maintain their union with the mother country.

But more than a little fire was evident in Jay's words, as he went on to warn the British of the consequences should they fail to allow the colonists their rights. If the British did not

When the First Continental Congress met in September 1774, as depicted here in this late eighteenth-century painting by Clyde O. Deland, the delegates did not, at the time, necessarily see it as a step toward the colonies' break away from Britain. Rather, they saw the congress as a one-time meeting to make Britain realize its mistakes in its treatment of the colonies. Jay at this time may have thought of himself as a Loyalist. The delegates' first order of business upon arriving in Philadelphia was getting to know one another. Many delegates had never traveled outside their colonies.

elect a parliament of "wisdom, independence and public spirit," he cautioned, and persisted on a course that would lead to war, they would pay a heavy price. If "neither the voice of justice, the dictates of the law, the principles of the constitution, or the suggestions of humanity can restrain your hands from shedding blood in such an impious cause," he wrote, Britain should beware, for "we will never submit to be hewers of wood or drawers of water for any ministry or nation in the world." Like his countrymen, Jay was moving steadily but implacably toward independence.

CHAPTER
3

THE DIPLOMAT

For Jay, as for his country, the die was now cast. Events moved quickly, seemingly of their own momentum. In late April 1775, British troops were sent to the Massachusetts towns of Lexington and Concord to investigate reports that colonial militias there—the minutemen—were stockpiling weapons. There, the redcoats and the minutemen clashed, and the "shot heard 'round the world" marked the beginning of the Revolutionary War. The Continental Congress quickly began the work of raising a military force, the Continental army, appointing George Washington as its commander-in-chief. In July 1776, the congress took an

In *General George Washington Resigning His Commission, 1783*, American soldier, diplomat, and painter John Trumbull portrayed one of the most important moments in the fate of America. Here, George Washington *(center)* is addressing Congress, which, on December 23, 1783, met in the Maryland State House in Annapolis. Washington resigns as commander in chief of the army, establishing that America would then be under civilian rule rather than military rule, after gaining its independence from Britain. His wife, Martha, and grandchildren are depicted watching from the gallery. They were not actually present at the time.

even more irrevocable step when it formally adopted the Declaration of Independence, written by Thomas Jefferson.

Until the summer of 1776, Jay himself, as a member of the Continental Congress, continued to hope and press for reconciliation with Britain. He was not present in Philadelphia in July 1776 when the congress voted for independence. However, it was assumed by his colleagues there that he would have voted against independence, as did, indeed, the New York delegation. But just several days later, Jay was in White Plains, New York, for the opening meeting of New York's Provincial Congress. This meeting had convened in response to congress's recommendation that each of the colonies create their own new governments as independent states. With a fleet of 100 British warships carrying 10,000 soldiers anchored just 20 miles (32 km) away in New York Harbor, Jay proposed that the New York Congress "join with the other colonies in supporting" the Declaration of Independence. They were doing so, Jay wrote, at the risk of their "lives and fortunes," because "cruel necessity" had made such a step "unavoidable." His resolution was adopted unanimously.

SERVING THE REVOLUTION

Once committed to the cause, Jay served the Revolution in a variety of ways. He worked to secure the defense of the vital Hudson River by obtaining cannon for its various fortresses. He met with Washington to discuss the state of the Continental army, the general's plans for defending the northern colonies, and the obtaining of reinforcements. He was the single most important individual in writing the constitution for the independent state of New York, also serving as the state's first chief justice (the judge responsible for overseeing its judiciary system). He even found time, while with the New York Provincial

The first and foremost impression that George Washington gave was that of a soldier, and he often wore his uniform. This painting by James Peale (brother of the painter Charles Peale) depicts General Washington at the Battle of Yorktown. Upon meeting him for the first time at the first Continental Congress, the other delegates were impressed with his stature, strength, and steady calm. It was rumored at the time of the Continental Congress that Washington had offered to raise and lead an army at his own expense.

Congress in the village of Fishkill, in Dutchess County, to oversee spy operations against the British. His escapades in this regard formed the basis for James Fenimore Cooper's 1821 novel, *The Spy*, which was wildly popular and hailed as one of the first real works of distinctly American literature.

The increased level of Jay's commitment was evident in the December 1776 publication of his "Address of the

This nineteenth-century depiction of the leaders of the Second Continental Congress includes, from left to right, John Adams, Gouverneur Morris, Alexander Hamilton, and Thomas Jefferson, possibly working out a draft of the Articles of Confederation. It became clear that there would be no reconciliation with England, and it was necessary to outline and create a union of the states and the power and responsibilities of each.

Convention of the Representatives of the State of New York to Their Constituents." The early fighting in the war had gone poorly for the Americans, with Washington's army being routed from New York City, but Jay pleaded with the people to remain united in their cause. He also urged Americans to forget about reconciliation and the idea that Britain desired peace. "If there be one single idea of peace in his [King George's] mind," he wrote, "why does he order your cities to be burned, your country to be desolated, your brethren to starve, and languish and die in prison?"

THE PRESIDENT OF THE CONTINENTAL CONGRESS

In December 1778, Jay was elected by the Continental Congress as its president. Some credited his election to the desire of the congress to have anyone from New York as its head for various political reasons. But Gouverneur Morris, a member of the New York delegation and not a particular admirer of Jay's, wrote that "the weight of [Jay's] personal character contributed as much to the election as the respect for the state." Even Samuel Adams, one of the congress's most radical delegates, voted for Jay.

The position was in some ways a frustrating one for Jay. It brought with it some prestige, a great deal of responsibility, and very little real authority. Congress had no power to levy taxes in order to raise funds for its operations, including maintaining the Continental army. To that extent, the congress was totally dependent upon the states. Besides cajoling, pleading, and attempting to sway, it had very few methods with which to persuade the individual states to comply with its wishes.

Jay's chief daily duty was to preside over the congress's deliberations, where he impressed all factions with his dignified impartiality. An even more significant responsibility was for correspondence—writing and reading letters to and from the various state governments so that both correspondents could keep abreast of the war's developments. Correspondence was also maintained with foreign dignitaries in order to assess prospects for aid, alliances, and peace negotiations. Perhaps his most important correspondence was with George Washington. This allowed Jay to assess the situation in the field; learn about the army's need; and assure Washington of the congress's continued support, even if it was often unable to provide all that was needed in terms of supplies, equipment, and funding. It was at this time that Jay developed his close and trusting relationship with Washington.

JAY IN PARIS

Jay performed his greatest service for the Revolution overseas when he spearheaded the negotiations that ended the war and secured England's recognition of the independent United States. In September 1779, he was asked by the Continental

This is a detail of the painting of a scene in Paris, France, created in 1777, by French painter Nicholas Jean-Baptiste Raguenet (1715–1793) titled *Le Pont Neuf et la Pompe de la Samaritaine, vus du quai de la Megisserie* (The Pont [Bridge] Neuf and Pumping Station of the Samaritaine from the View of the Megisseire). At this time, Paris was the largest city in Europe with half a million people. There existed a stark contrast between the rich and poor, as well as contrasts between its narrow, dirty streets and classical buildings, fountains, and open spaces.

Congress to lead a diplomatic mission to Spain to ask that nation for financial assistance with the war. He sailed the following month, accompanied by Sarah and their young son, Peter. (The couple would have five more children in the years to come.) Months of negotiation with Spain proved fruitless, but by the beginning of 1782 Jay had been summoned to Paris by Benjamin Franklin. In October 1781, Britain had been made to surrender to Washington and his French allies—who constituted nearly half the rebel force—at the Battle of Yorktown in Virginia. Now Britain was ready to negotiate peace terms with the United States.

Jay faced a tricky task in France, which had been providing the United States with major military and financial assistance, including most of the Continental army's guns and almost all of its gunpowder, since 1778. (The American victory at the Battle of Saratoga in the autumn of 1777 apparently convinced the French that the Americans could actually win the war.) The treaty of assistance between the United States and France stated that the former would not negotiate a separate peace with England.

But in Paris, Jay came to agree with John Adams (the other important member, with Franklin, of the peace commission delegated by the Continental Congress) that French and U.S. interests no longer exactly coincided. France, Adams believed, wanted to negotiate a peace that left the United States independent but not too strong, while the United States was obviously interested in obtaining the best terms that it could. The wily and worldly French foreign minister, the Comte de Vergennes, also worried that as neophytes in international diplomacy, the Americans would simply be outclassed by the experienced British negotiators.

The American delegation, especially Jay and Adams, had no such doubts. Jay successfully insisted on British recognition of the United States' independence as a sovereign nation as a prerequisite to the talks. This resulted in the Americans opening separate negotiations with the British. Within several months, the Treaty of Paris had been written, conceding to the Americans the most important points on which they had insisted: independence, of course, and the establishment of the country's western borders at the Mississippi River.

Franklin, Adams, and, Most Fortunately, the Presence of Jay

Jay's most impressive feat of diplomacy may have come with the members of his own delegation. Franklin and Adams were both brilliant men, with powerful but very different personalities. Franklin had been famous in Europe since the 1750s for his experiments with electricity. Since 1776, Franklin had been in Paris trying to gain French support for the American cause. He was lionized as the "first American" by the French, who took to him for his wit, high spirits that belied his age (Franklin was in his seventies by this time), his passionate irreverence, and his obvious affection for the French themselves and their way of life. For the French, Franklin fulfilled their idea of an authentic American. They saw him as a pure embodiment of the republican spirit and

The American Peace Commissioners, by Benjamin West from 1783, was meant to be a depiction of all those involved in the peace negotiations in Paris. However, West only completed painting the Americans involved in signing the treaty with Great Britain. It is believed the British commissioners refused to sit for the portrait. From left to right: John Jay, John Adams, Benjamin Franklin, Henry Laurens, and William Temple Franklin, who acted as secretary.

intellectual energies of the new nation and a man who also seemed to embrace the most crucial elements of their own Enlightenment—reason as the best arbiter of human affairs, the spirit of scientific inquiry, and faith in human progress.

Adams was a more difficult case. Besides a few short breaks, he had been in Paris with Franklin continuously since 1778. There, the two men succeeded in negotiating the treaty that provided France's support for the Revolution. The best-read and most prolific writer of any of the public figures of his generation, Adams was also insecure, opinionated, quick-tongued, and pompous. While in Paris, he began developing what would ultimately amount to an obsession: he believed that he would be denied his proper share of credit for the Revolution by Franklin, whom he was convinced had developed a dislike for him. "I knew [Franklin] had conceived an irreconcilable hatred to me and that he had propagated and would continue to propagate prejudices, if nothing worse, against me in America from one end of it to the other," Adams later wrote in an April 12, 1809, letter to his friend Dr. Benjamin Rush.

It would not be surprising if Franklin had developed a dislike for Adams; given enough time and exposure, most people did. Franklin's famous characterization of Adams, included in a letter Franklin wrote on July 22, 1783, to Robert Livingston, is one with which most of his contemporaries would have concurred: "He means well for his country, is always an honest man, often a wise one, but sometimes and in some things, absolutely out of his senses." While Franklin had something of a genius for personal relationships, Adams was more masterful at alienating people.

Their differences extended even to diplomatic style. To Adams, Franklin seemed never to be working; he seemed instead always to be attending or rising late from society balls, fashionable salons, dinner engagements, and the like, where he was invariably the center of attention. For Franklin, Adams's style lacked subtlety; his idea of negotiating seemed to be to harangue the representatives of England and France with an unyielding barrage of points, conditions, and demands.

By winning the friendship of both, Jay was able to draw on their strong points for success in the peace talks. He recognized that Adams was more familiar than Franklin with what specific points in the talks—such as access to the rich cod fisheries of Canada—were of most practical importance to Americans back at home, particularly to Adams's fellow New Englanders. He learned quickly to rely on Adams's command of detail. He recognized also that Franklin's seemingly more cavalier approach actually reflected a sophisticated appreciation of the nuances of European-style diplomacy. This was diplomacy that could turn as much on matters of personality, style, and relationships as it did on hard bargaining over a table. While enjoying the Parisian nightlife, Jay realized, Franklin was also working; connections forged, gossip gathered, observations

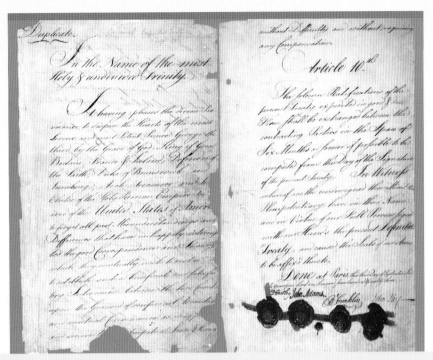

The Paris Peace Treaty of 1783, bearing the signature and wax seals of arms of each of its signers: D. Hartley (representing George III), John Adams, B. Franklin, and John Jay, laid out such terms as the British recognition of the thirteen colonies as the United States of America, payment of debts, the releasing of all prisoners of war, and each nation's rightful access to the Mississippi River.

made in Paris's salons and restaurants could prove invaluable in the negotiations.

But Jay's contribution was something the two men could agree on. Franklin was so impressed by Jay's character and trustworthiness that he named Jay as one of the executors of his will. In his journal, Adams confided that it was Jay, even more than himself, who deserved most of the credit for the treaty. Jay, Adams wrote, deserved to be remembered as the "George

Washington" of the negotiations. Typically, Jay himself was less concerned with receiving credit than he was with hopes for his country. "We are now thank God in full possession of peace and independence," he wrote in a letter home. "If we are not a happy people now it will be our own fault."

CHAPTER
4

THE FEDERALIST

J ay returned to the United States in July 1784 to serve as secretary of foreign affairs for the Continental Congress, a position he maintained until 1790. In his new post, Jay was the top foreign policy adviser for the congress. Chiefly, this meant he met and corresponded with foreign ambassadors and dignitaries and kept the congress informed of the state of these relationships. He was also responsible for urging the individual states to honor the terms of the treaties that the congress entered into on their behalf.

As he had while serving as president of the Continental Congress, Jay found the position frustrating.

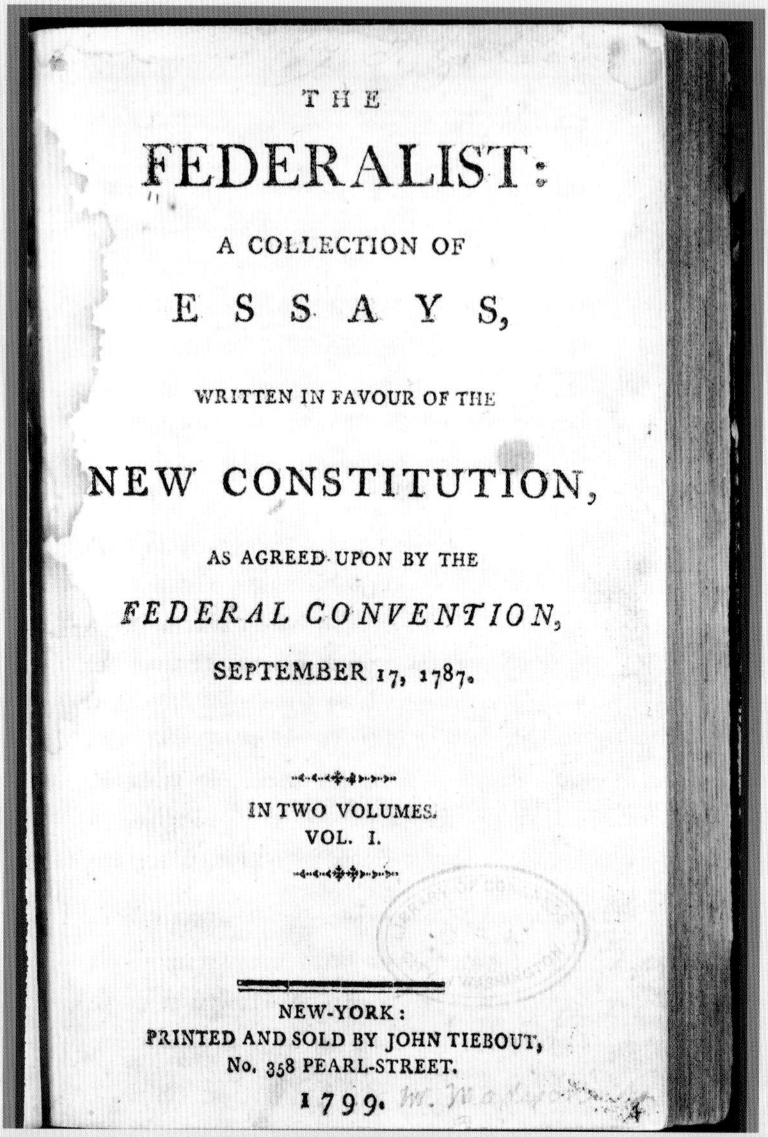

THE

FEDERALIST:

A COLLECTION OF

E S S A Y S,

WRITTEN IN FAVOUR OF THE

NEW CONSTITUTION,

AS AGREED UPON BY THE

FEDERAL CONVENTION,

SEPTEMBER 17, 1787.

IN TWO VOLUMES.
VOL. I.

NEW-YORK:
PRINTED AND SOLD BY JOHN TIEBOUT,
No. 358 PEARL-STREET.
1799.

Seen here is the cover of the 1799 edition of *The Federalist*, as the essays penned by Hamilton, Madison, and Jay in support of the Constitution were known. While publicly supportive, Jay privately expressed misgivings about certain provisions of the Constitution, such as those giving the federal government supremacy over the states and requiring a two-thirds approval of the Senate for ratification of foreign treaties.

The Articles of Confederation had been drafted by the congress in 1777 and formally adopted by all the individual states in 1781. This "firm league of friendship" defined how the congress was to be responsible for the foreign affairs of the United States, with most other powers reserved for the individual states. As the chief architect of the Treaty of Paris, Jay was especially troubled that many of the states did not comply with the terms of the treaty, especially those provisions that called for the repayment of commercial debts owed to the British.

A Need for Stronger Government

Congress could not force such compliance. Neither could it respond meaningfully to such events as Shays's Rebellion, an armed revolt by debt-ridden veterans and farmers in western Massachusetts. This led Jay to conclude that the United States needed a stronger form of government. Many others were drawing the same conclusion. Though they would later divide over some of the practical questions of government, Washington, Hamilton, Madison, and even Jefferson agreed that the Articles of Confederation needed to be strengthened or replaced.

Jay corresponded with each of these men about the matter. His recommendation was essentially the same as theirs: a strong federal government that divided powers between the

This painting, titled *Scene at the Signing of the Constitution of the United States*, shows how the scene at Independence Hall in Philadelphia, on September 17, 1787, was imagined by American artist Howard Chandler Christy in 1940. George Washington *(standing, right)* is about to sign the Constitution at the desk. Of the fifty-five delegates to the Convention, only thirty-nine are depicted here. Christy did not include the delegates who had left the convention or did not sign the Constitution.

executive, legislative, and judiciary branches. In a letter to Jefferson during the summer of 1786, Jay explained that he had "long thought and become more daily convinced that the construction of our federal government was fundamentally wrong. To vest legislative, judicial and executive powers in one and the same body of men . . . can never be wise. In my opinion, those three great departments of sovereignty should be forever separated, and so distributed as to serve as checks on each other." To Washington in a letter at the same time, Jay put it even more simply: "Let Congress legislate. Let others execute. Let others judge."

Primarily at the instigation of Hamilton and Madison, the Constitutional Convention was held in Philadelphia in May 1787. Its proceedings were to be held in secret. Officially, the convention was being held "for the sole and express purpose of revising the Articles of

Confederation," but men like Hamilton, Madison, and Jay had already decided that they were going to replace the Articles with a new constitution.

NEW CHALLENGES, NEW DIVIDES

Every state but Rhode Island sent delegates to the Constitutional Convention, which was attended by fifty-five delegates in all. Among those present were Washington; Hamilton; Madison; and, in a wheelchair, the eighty-one-year-old Benjamin Franklin. Perhaps equally impressive was the list of those who were unable or unwilling to attend. These included Richard Henry Lee, Patrick Henry, Thomas Jefferson, John Adams, Samuel Adams, and John Hancock.

Jay was both able and presumably willing to attend, but he was not chosen as one of New York's three delegates. Although not physically in attendance, he was nonetheless a presence in Philadelphia. He had worked closely in the past with all of the

The original United States Constitution is permanently displayed in Washington, D.C., at the National Archives. The U.S. government as described by the Constitution went into effect on March 4, 1789. Rhode Island sent no delegates to the convention and was the last state to ratify the document. One heated debate during the creation of the Constitution was about the number of representatives in the legislature for each state. Larger states wanted representation to be based on population, but smaller states wanted an equal number for all.

We the People

of the United States, in Order to form a more perfect Union, establish Justice, insure domestic Tranquility, provide for the common defence, promote the general Welfare, and secure the Blessings of Liberty to ourselves and our Posterity, do ordain and establish this Constitution for the United States of America.

Article. I.

Section. 1. All legislative Powers herein granted shall be vested in a Congress of the United States, which shall consist of a Senate and House of Representatives.

Section. 2. The House of Representatives shall be composed of Members chosen every second Year by the People of the several States, and the Electors in each State shall have the Qualifications requisite for Electors of the most numerous Branch of the State Legislature.

No Person shall be a Representative who shall not have attained to the Age of twenty five Years, and been seven Years a Citizen of the United States, and who shall not, when elected, be an Inhabitant of that State in which he shall be chosen.

Representatives and direct Taxes shall be apportioned among the several States which may be included within this Union, according to their respective Numbers, which shall be determined by adding to the whole Number of free Persons, including those bound to Service for a Term of Years, and excluding Indians not taxed, three fifths of all other Persons. The actual Enumeration shall be made within three Years after the first Meeting of the Congress of the United States, and within every subsequent Term of ten Years, in such Manner as they shall by Law direct. The Number of Representatives shall not exceed one for every thirty Thousand, but each State shall have at Least one Representative; and until such enumeration shall be made, the State of New Hampshire shall be entitled to chuse three, Massachusetts eight, Rhode Island and Providence Plantations one, Connecticut five, New York six, New Jersey four, Pennsylvania eight, Delaware one, Maryland six, Virginia ten, North Carolina five, South Carolina five, and Georgia three.

When vacancies happen in the Representation from any State, the Executive Authority thereof shall issue Writs of Election to fill such Vacancies.

The House of Representatives shall chuse their Speaker and other Officers; and shall have the sole Power of Impeachment.

Section. 3. The Senate of the United States shall be composed of two Senators from each State, chosen by the Legislature thereof, for six Years; and each Senator shall have one Vote.

Immediately after they shall be assembled in Consequence of the first Election, they shall be divided as equally as may be into three Classes. The Seats of the Senators of the first Class shall be vacated at the Expiration of the second Year, of the second Class at the Expiration of the fourth Year, and of the third Class at the Expiration of the sixth Year, so that one third may be chosen every second Year; and if Vacancies happen by Resignation, or otherwise, during the Recess of the Legislature of any State, the Executive thereof may make temporary Appointments until the next Meeting of the Legislature, which shall then fill such Vacancies.

No Person shall be a Senator who shall not have attained to the Age of thirty Years, and been nine Years a Citizen of the United States, and who shall not, when elected, be an Inhabitant of that State for which he shall be chosen.

The Vice President of the United States shall be President of the Senate, but shall have no Vote, unless they be equally divided.

The Senate shall chuse their other Officers, and also a President pro tempore, in the Absence of the Vice President, or when he shall exercise the Office of President of the United States.

The Senate shall have the sole Power to try all Impeachments. When sitting for that Purpose, they shall be on Oath or Affirmation. When the President of the United States is tried, the Chief Justice shall preside: And no Person shall be convicted without the Concurrence of two thirds of the Members present.

Judgment in Cases of Impeachment shall not extend further than to removal from Office, and disqualification to hold and enjoy any Office of honor, Trust or Profit under the United States: but the Party convicted shall nevertheless be liable and subject to Indictment, Trial, Judgment and Punishment, according to Law.

Section. 4. The Times, Places and Manner of holding Elections for Senators and Representatives, shall be prescribed in each State by the Legislature thereof; but the Congress may at any time by Law make or alter such Regulations, except as to the Places of chusing Senators.

The Congress shall assemble at least once in every Year, and such Meeting shall be on the first Monday in December, unless they shall by Law appoint a different Day.

Section. 5. Each House shall be the Judge of the Elections, Returns and Qualifications of its own Members, and a Majority of each shall constitute a Quorum to do Business; but a smaller Number may adjourn from day to day, and may be authorized to compel the Attendance of absent Members, in such Manner, and under such Penalties as each House may provide.

Each House may determine the Rules of its Proceedings, punish its Members for disorderly Behaviour, and, with the Concurrence of two thirds, expel a Member.

Each House shall keep a Journal of its Proceedings, and from time to time publish the same, excepting such Parts as may in their Judgment require Secrecy; and the Yeas and Nays of the Members of either House on any question shall, at the Desire of one fifth of those Present, be entered on the Journal.

Neither House, during the Session of Congress, shall, without the Consent of the other, adjourn for more than three days, nor to any other Place than that in which the two Houses shall be sitting.

Section. 6. The Senators and Representatives shall receive a Compensation for their Services, to be ascertained by Law, and paid out of the Treasury of the United States. They shall in all Cases, except Treason, Felony and Breach of the Peace, be privileged from Arrest during their Attendance at the Session of their respective Houses, and in going to and returning from the same; and for any Speech or Debate in either House, they shall not be questioned in any other Place.

No Senator or Representative shall, during the Time for which he was elected, be appointed to any civil Office under the Authority of the United States, which shall have been created, or the Emoluments whereof shall have been encreased during such time; and no Person holding most important delegates to the convention, and he kept up with the convention's deliberations and made sure his own ideas were heard through his frequent correspondence, especially with Washington.

The Constitution drafted in the summer of 1787 provided a new government for the United States essentially along the lines Jay had hoped: a strong federal government divided into three branches—the executive, headed by an elected president; the legislative, which consisted of two elected assemblies, the Senate and the House of Representatives; and the judiciary, or court system. Each branch possessed checks and balances on the powers and privileges of the other branches, ensuring that the new government would possess the balance that the Founding Fathers believed was the essence of good government.

Most important, from Jay's point of view, was the so-called supremacy clause of the new Constitution. It stated that the new Constitution, and any treaties and laws enacted under it, "shall be the supreme law of the land," regardless of the law of the individual states. Jay and his fellow Federalists, as supporters of the Constitution were known, were pleased that the national government of the United States at last had the power it needed to govern effectively.

Now, the challenge for the Federalists became to persuade their fellow Americans to adopt, or ratify, the new Constitution. Conventions to debate ratification were called in each of the thirteen states. The Constitution was to be considered adopted as the "supreme law of the land" if nine of the thirteen states voted to ratify it, but the leading Federalists considered it extremely important that adoption be as close to unanimous as possible. No one was quite sure how or if a state could be made to abide by the new Constitution, especially if the state was one of the largest and most important, such as Virginia or New York. The Federalists were not eager to face this issue, which would have provoked an immediate constitutional crisis right from the outset of the new system.

There was no guarantee that such a crisis could be avoided. Sixteen of the fifty-five delegates to the Constitutional Convention had refused to sign the finished document, including a majority of the Virginia and New York delegates. Both of those states were assumed to be anti-Federalist. Indeed, the prevailing anti-Federalist sentiment in New York was probably the reason Jay had not been asked to be a member of the state's delegation to the Constitutional Convention.

THE FEDERALIST PAPERS

But Virginia and New York were also home to three of the most prominent and articulate Federalists–Madison, Hamilton, and Jay. Within no more than a week or so of the end of the Constitutional Convention in late September 1787, Hamilton conceived the idea of writing and publishing a series of essays

For the Independent Journal.

The FŒDERALIST. No. I.

To the People of the State of New-York.

AFTER an unequivocal experience of the inefficacy of the subsisting Fœderal Government, you are called upon to deliberate on a new Constitution for the United States of America. The subject speaks its own importance; comprehending in its consequences, nothing less than the existence of the UNION, the safety and welfare of the parts of which it is composed, the fate of an empire, in many respects, the most interesting in the world. It has been frequently remarked, that it seems to have been reserved to the people of this country, by their conduct and example, to decide the important question, whether societies of men are really capable or not, of establishing good government from reflection and choice, or whether they are forever destined to depend, for their political constitutions, on accident and force. If there be any truth in the remark, the crisis, at which we are arrived, may with propriety be regarded as the æra in which that decision is to be made; and a wrong election of the part we shall act, may, in this view, deserve to be considered as the general misfortune of mankind.

This idea will add the inducements of philanthropy to those of patriotism to heighten the sollicitude, which all considerate and good men must feel for the event. Happy will it be if our choice should be decided by a judicious estimate of our true interests, unperplexed and unbiassed by considerations not connected with the public good. But this is a thing more ardently to be wished, than seriously to be expected. The plan offered to our deliberations, affects too many particular interests, innovates upon too many local institutions, not to involve in its discussion a variety of objects foreign to its merits, and of views, passions and prejudices little favourable to the discovery in New York newspapers for the purpose of influencing public opinion in favor of the Constitution. These essays, known as the Federalist Papers, were initially to number no more than twenty to twenty-five.

Ultimately, eighty-four Federalist essays would appear in the press, eighty-five in the book collection that was published shortly afterward as *The Federalist*. All of the essays were published anonymously, under the pseudonym Publius, which was short for Publius Valerius, a citizen of ancient Rome who had helped establish the Roman republic after the overthrow of the monarchy. Taken together, Madison wrote to Washington, the Federalist Papers "present a full discussion of the merits of the proposed Constitution in all its relations." As such, they became well known in all the states, not just New York, as the Constitution's ratification was considered. They remain today among the most important primary documents in U.S. history, an unmatched revelation of what the architects of the Constitution hoped to accomplish.

The first of what would collectively be known as *The Federalist*, "The Federalist No. 1," written by Hamilton, is pictured here as it appeared in the *New-York Independent Journal* on October 21, 1787. One interesting opposition to the Constitution and very much emphasized in *The Federalist* was the opposition to a bill of rights. This was because if a bill of rights of the people was included, it could be interpreted as their only rights. However, in "The Federalist No. 1," Hamilton only outlines how "Publius," the pen name used by *The Federalist* authors, plans to persuade his countrymen in the course of these articles of the utmost importance of accepting the proposed Constitution.

Hamilton's arguments in *The Federalist* relied on his belief that given the proper arguments, logic, and rationale, his audience would inevitably be won over to the rightness of his position. He also realized the importance of New York to the ratification of the Constitution—given its geographical location and economic might, New York's failure to ratify might undo the new union of states.

Hamilton was an incredibly prolific writer, but he recognized that he could not handle writing the Federalist Papers by himself. His first choice for a collaborator was Jay, who immediately agreed to join the project. Madison was then asked to join them. Hamilton, Jay, and Madison divided the task between them, with each writing a number of essays on his own. They did not collaborate on individual essays. Though it was generally known at the time that Hamilton, Jay, and Madison were Publius, who wrote which essay was not as widely known.

As historians have since been able to determine which writer wrote which essay, we know today that Jay wrote only

James Madison shared Hamilton's views regarding New York's importance in ratifying the Constitution. Thus, Madison was easily persuaded by Hamilton to help him with *The Federalist* project. Madison's thinking on the Constitution was greatly influenced by French political thinker Charles de Secondat, Baron de Montesquieu's theories on the separation of powers in government.

five of the essays, numbers 2, 3, 4, 5, and 64. Most likely, both Jay and Hamilton intended for Jay to take a larger role in the authorship, but after writing essays 2 through 5, he became severely ill in November 1787. This was probably due to rheumatoid arthritis. Jay was unable to work again until the spring, when he penned his final contribution. In Jay's absence, Hamilton and Madison then completed the rest of the writing.

Jay's essays are generally considered the weakest contributions to *The Federalist*, which was regarded then and now as primarily the work of Hamilton and Madison. Indeed, Jay's contributions were so little recognized at the time that in November 1787, widespread reports appeared in the press stating that he had become an anti-Federalist. His essays largely emphasized the ways that a strengthened government under the Constitution would make it easier for the United States to conduct its foreign affairs and make it safer from war. This is not surprising, considering Jay's concerns as president of the Continental Congress and secretary for foreign affairs under the Articles of Confederation.

A DIRECT APPEAL TO NEW YORKERS

More persuasive in the debate over the Constitution was Jay's "Address to the People of the State of New York," which was published anonymously as a pamphlet while he was recuperating from his bout with rheumatoid arthritis. Walter Stahr, Jay's sole contemporary biographer, calls it "the single most persuasive paper in the blizzard of paper produced in New York about the Constitution." Jay's contemporaries agreed. Washington expressed his admiration for the document in a letter dated May 15, 1788, writing that it would make "a serious impression even upon the Antifederal mind." Their mutual friend John Vaughn informed Jay by letter in June 1788 that Franklin believed Jay should let people know that he was the author, believing that in so doing Jay "would give it additional weight at this awful crisis."

In his address, Jay urged Americans to adopt the Constitution in the same spirit of revolutionary unity in which they had acted against the British. Doing so, he wrote, was "to continue to move and act as they [previously] have done, as a Band of Brothers; to continue to have confidence in themselves and one other."

By the time *The Federalist* was published in book form on May 28, 1788, eight of the thirteen states had ratified the Constitution. Within a month, New Hampshire joined them, making the Constitution the "supreme law of the land." Ratification by Virginia and New York came by the end of July, with North Carolina's approval coming a year later. Rhode Island, always the last holdout, ratified the Constitution in May 1790, making it unanimous. For John Adams, it was Jay who deserved most of the credit. When it came to devising the Constitution and securing its ratification, Adams wrote in his journal, Jay was "of more importance than any of the rest, indeed of almost as much weight as the rest."

CHAPTER
5

THE MOST HATED MAN IN AMERICA

A s all had expected during the debates over the Constitution, George Washington was unanimously elected president. He quickly made the four most important appointments to his new government. Thomas Jefferson was chosen as secretary of state, head of the department responsible for conducting the nation's foreign affairs. Alexander Hamilton was selected as secretary of the treasury, head of the department responsible for overseeing the nation's finances. Henry Knox was chosen as secretary of war, head of the department responsible for the nation's defense. And John Jay was named as first chief justice of the Supreme

This is a portrait of John Jay as first chief justice of the U.S. Supreme Court by American painter Gilbert Stuart. Jay sat for the portrait, but left before its completion for his assignment as envoy to England. Jay's wife, Sarah, pushed Stuart to complete it in Jay's absence and was extremely happy with the completed work, considering it a masterpiece that could not be re-created. There was much speculation as to who Washington would appoint in his most senior positions. Jay was offered the position as secretary of the treasury, but he was not interested. He preferred the position of chief justice, and his main concern and goal was to ensure the proper repayment of debts to British creditors in order to prevent a second war.

Court, which meant he was the most important judge of the highest court of the land as well as the man responsible for overseeing the new federal judicial system.

Jay served as chief justice through Washington's first term as president and into his second when, in the spring of 1794, Washington asked him to go to England as special envoy. That request alone indicates that the position of chief justice was very different from what it is today, when it would be unthinkable for a president to ask a chief justice to step down to carry out a political mission, no matter how important. As the first chief justice, Jay was less responsible for presiding over the Court's hearing of cases than he was for getting the federal judicial system up and running. (It was not until the term of the fourth chief justice, John Marshall, that the U.S. Supreme Court issued its first historically significant ruling. In that case, *Marbury v. Madison*, the Court established the principles of judicial review, which is the judicial branch's most important power. Under judicial review, the judicial branch has the authority to review the acts of the other two branches of government to determine if they are constitutional.)

AMERICA AND THE FRENCH REVOLUTION

Washington asked Jay to go to England in the hope that Jay's gift for diplomacy could help resolve the foreign policy crisis that was the most important issue of his own two terms as well as the presidency of John Adams.

The crisis was the problematic relationship between the United States, France, and Great Britain. Yet it was also a domestic crisis, raising tremendous passion and emotion in the states. Indeed, it hardened differences of opinion among the Revolution's "Band of Brothers" and generated the country's first political parties. In many ways, the crisis was the culmination of the dispute that began over the Constitution. At stake was nothing less than the true meaning of the American Revolution and the future direction and shape of the U.S. government.

At the same time that the United States was establishing its new system of government under the Constitution, France was undergoing its own revolution. First the monarchy was overthrown, followed by the hereditary nobility and aristocracy that had been the basis for its own government. During the so-called Reign of Terror, both the king and queen and many members of the aristocracy were executed, and the church's role in public affairs was also undone.

As the revolution progressed in France, its traditional enemy, England, grew alarmed that revolutionary sentiment would spread across Europe and even to England itself. This would give France increased influence and possibly even lead to revolution in England. Thus, England responded by declaring war on France and seeking to prevent other nations from trading

Destruction of the Emblems of the Monarchy, Place de la Concorde, August 10, 1793, by Pierre-Antoine Demachy. The years of the French Revolution span from 1789 to 1799. At first, Jay and many other Americans thought the revolution showed much promise. However, the execution of Louis XVI and Queen Marie Antoinette caused Jay and many others to conclude that the revolution had taken an unacceptably lawless and murderous course. The French Revolution marked a turning point in European history, from the age of absolute monarchy to the exercise of power by the people.

with it. In the case of the United States, this meant forcibly boarding and seizing American ships and cargoes bound for France. France soon responded in kind and began treating American shipping the same way.

These events reverberated in the United States. Many Americans, most famously such prominent figures as Thomas Jefferson and the radical pamphleteer Thomas Paine, saw the events as the logical culmination of what they had begun with

America's Revolution. Indeed, many French revolutionaries saw Jefferson, Paine, and Franklin as inspiration in their own fight for liberty. By this interpretation, the American Revolution had been about not just independence from Britain, but a first step for liberty in general. By this they meant an end to monarchy and aristocracy as a basis for government. It was a necessary first strike against what the French regarded as the "superstition" and "ignorance" of organized religion. Those sympathetic to the French Revolution also cited France's aid to the United States during its revolution as reason for that support to be returned now.

Men such as Washington, Adams, Hamilton, and Jay himself were horrified by the events in France. They regarded its supporters as holding a radical and mistaken interpretation of the meaning of the American Revolution, which, as both Adams and Jay would state, had been a matter of necessity and pride, not liberty. As Adams explained it (and Jay agreed with him), the American Revolution did not take place because the Americans had any fundamental quarrel with the form of the British government, which they understood as a monarchy with shared powers with the legislative and judicial branches. According to this view, all the Americans were asking for was their fundamental rights under the British constitution. (The British had long considered themselves as governed by a constitution. Yet their constitution consisted not of a written document, like the American one, but of a tradition of principles

The scholar, idealist, and radical pamphleteer Thomas Paine advocated independence from Britain in his most famous work, *Common Sense*, even influencing George Washington on the issue. His strong support of the French Revolution led to his involvement as a representative at its national convention. However, Paine's opposition to capital punishment led him to support King Louis XVI's exile to America, and he was imprisoned by the revolution's radical leadership.

and precedents from British history.) The Americans had been denied those rights not because of any inherent flaw in the British system, but because that system had become "corrupted." The system had become unbalanced between the various branches of government, with too much power shifting toward the executive (the king) and away from the legislative, which included within it the representatives of the aristocracy in the form of Parliament's upper house, the House of Lords.

From this point of view, the American Revolution and its aftermath, including the establishment of the Constitution, had been less an advance of liberty and a blow against the

British form of government. Rather, it had been an expression of grievances against specific British policies and a rooting out of the corruption that had caused the British system to malfunction. Indeed, the leading Federalists, such as Jay, Adams, Hamilton, and Washington, believed that the greatness of the U.S. Constitution was that it essentially replicated the best features of the British form of government, with some crucial adjustments. Adams even referred to the "monarchical, aristocratical, and democratical" branches of the U.S. government. By this he meant the presidency, the Senate (whose members were not, under the original Constitution, directly elected by the people), and the House of Representatives (whose members were elected).

For reasons such as these, the Federalists favored closer ties with Britain. The French Revolution scared them as a dangerously "foreign," radical, and mistaken by-product of the American Revolution. Among the Federalists, Hamilton especially supported Great Britain for practical reasons as well, arguing that England was the United States' traditional and "natural" trading partner by reasons of language, culture, and history.

THE ANTI-FEDERALISTS

The great fear of the anti-Federalists, who were soon to be more commonly referred to as Republicans, was that the Constitution was a means of strengthening the power of the central government at the expense of their own rights. They feared a restoration of the kind of "tyranny" that had made the American Revolution necessary in the first place. Statements like Adams's that the colonists had had no quarrel with the "form" of the British government tended to confirm those fears, resulting in widespread accusations that Adams and Washington were actually secret monarchists. In this sense, support for Britain in its quarrels with revolutionary France seemed to the anti-Federalists to be a betrayal of the sacred cause of the American Revolution, as well as a betrayal of America's great ally, France. The Federalists were thus seen as the enemies of liberty, while they themselves viewed anti-Federalists as dangerous fanatics and radicals.

Jay's Mission

It was against this backdrop that Washington asked Jay to go to England. His mission was to persuade the English to sign a treaty with the United States allowing American shipping to go unhindered on the high seas. Washington hoped that Jay's success would help calm the vehement anti-British and anti-French sentiments in the United States. The Federalists feared these sentiments might force the United States into another war with Great Britain—a war for which the divided country was not prepared militarily or financially.

Jay burns in effigy following public disclosure of the terms of the treaty he had negotiated with Britain. Such demonstrations were a common sight across America in the spring and summer of 1795. Once Washington signed the treaty, however, people began to warm to it, as it was hard for Americans to criticize the president. Also, many Americans wanted to move west where British forts and Britain's Native American allies were present, making it risky to have tension with Britain.

Jay later wrote that he knew his mission was doomed to failure before he even left for England. His own sense of duty motivated him to carry on, but in any event he was decidedly pro-British. He had very little with which to gain concessions from the British, who were aware that the United States could not afford to fight. Although he did succeed in getting the British to agree to a treaty, it gave the United States nothing of what it wanted. Britain agreed to remove its troops from the western forts where they had remained since the Revolution, but it refused to stop seizing American ships.

Jay returned to New York City from London in May 1795. Copies of the treaty had preceded him across the

Atlantic. Recognizing its probable unpopularity, Washington had persuaded the Senate to begin considering the treaty in secret. With a strong Federalist majority in the Senate, the treaty was ratified in late June, but its actual terms were still kept secret. All that the newspapers were able to report was that the treaty had been ratified. This naturally enraged the Republicans, many of whom regarded the idea of any treaty with England as a betrayal of liberty and the American Revolution. In the absence of reliable information, wild rumors about the contents of the treaty began to spread. The secrecy of the deliberations was denounced as evidence of a British monarchical plot and the government's antidemocratic intentions.

THE AFTERMATH OF JAY'S TREATY

Then in early July, Benjamin Franklin Bache, grandson of the great Franklin himself and publisher of a fervently Republican Philadelphia newspaper, the *Aurora*, obtained a copy of the treaty and published it in his newspaper. The outcry against it was passionate, hostile, and immediate. Hamilton was stoned by an angry mob in New York City and the Jay Treaty was denounced across the country. Jay himself became the most hated man in America, burned in effigy in many cities and denounced publicly as a pro-British stooge and lackey. He later said that he could have ridden across the country at night by

Upon retirement from public life, Jay had this house built on the farm he had earlier purchased near Katonah, New York. It was here that he spent twenty-eight years of retirement before his death in 1829. Even before the Revolution, Jay had begun investing the profits from his law practice in several substantial tracts of real estate in southern New York state, which allowed him to enjoy his retirement in relative comfort.

the light from the bonfires where his effigy was being burned. To intense criticism, Washington approved the treaty. He later said that the passions and criticism that the treaty aroused helped persuade him not to seek a third term as president.

The treaty also effectively ended Jay's time on the national stage. He had been elected governor of New York while in England negotiating the treaty, and he served two terms in that post from 1795 to 1801. At the same time, he continued to act as an adviser to Washington. At Hamilton's request, he reviewed and edited Washington's Farewell Address, which Hamilton had written for the president.

The clamor over the Jay Treaty would not end the American conflict over Britain and France, which would grow even more tumultuous during Adams's only term as president. It would no longer, however, involve Jay. By now drawing near age sixty, increasingly troubled with rheumatoid arthritis and other illnesses, Jay was getting ready to withdraw from public life. When Adams asked him to serve once again as chief justice of the Supreme Court, Jay, for the first time in his life, refused his nation's call to duty. Instead, after finishing his second term as governor of New York, he retired, with Sarah, to the farm he had purchased near the present-day town of Katonah, New York, in north-central Westchester County. There, especially after the death of his beloved Sarah in 1802, he lived a quiet life of increasing solitude, withdrawing from all public affairs, until his own death on May 17, 1829.

TIMELINE

1664 England wrests New Amsterdam from the Netherlands and renames it New York.

1745 John Jay is born in New York City on December 12.

1753 Jay is sent to study at a private boarding school in New Rochelle, New York.

1760 Jay enrolls at King's College (later Columbia University) in New York City.

1763 Great Britain gains victory in the Seven Years' War.

1764 Jay graduates from King's College and begins studying to be a law clerk.

1765 Great Britain issues the Stamp Act for the thirteen colonies.

1767 Great Britain imposes the Townshend Acts on the thirteen colonies.

1768 Jay is admitted to the New York bar.

1770 The skirmish known as the Boston Massacre takes place on March 5.

1773 The Boston Tea Party occurs on the night of December 16.

(continued on following page)

(continued from previous page)

1774 Great Britain imposes the Intolerable Acts; Jay marries Sarah Livingston on April 28; the First Continental Congress meets in Philadelphia in September.

1775 Redcoats clash with minutemen at Lexington and Concord; George Washington assumes command of the Continental army.

1776 The Continental Congress approves the Declaration of Independence.

1777 Americans win a key victory over the British at the Battle of Saratoga.

1778 Jay begins service as president of the Continental Congress; Benjamin Franklin and John Adams secure military and financial aid from France for the United States.

1779 Jay sails for Europe on a diplomatic mission to Spain and France.

1781 A combined American and French force defeats the British at the Battle of Yorktown in Virginia.

1783 The United States and Great Britain formally agree upon the Treaty of Paris, ending the Revolutionary War.

1784 Jay returns to the United States and begins service as the secretary of foreign affairs for the Continental Congress.

1787 The Constitutional Convention meets in Philadelphia.

1788 *The Federalist* is completed, with Jay writing five essays; the U.S. Constitution is ratified.

1789 Washington is unanimously elected first president of the United States.

1790 Jay takes office as the first chief justice of the Supreme Court.

1794 Jay goes to London to negotiate a treaty with Great Britain.

1795 Jay's Treaty is approved, to great public outrage; Jay becomes governor of New York.

1797 John Adams becomes president; Jay helps Alexander Hamilton with writing Washington's Farewell Address.

1801 Jay retires from public life to a farm near Katonah, New York.

1829 Jay dies on May 17.

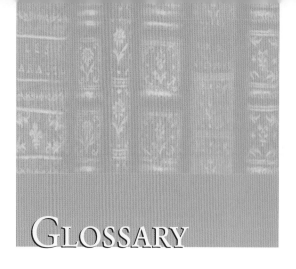

GLOSSARY

admonition A gentle warning or piece of advice.

affront An insult or offense.

aristocracy Government by a small, privileged class.

bastion Something that is considered a stronghold.

boycott An organized refusal to have dealings with an organization, store, or person.

charisma A personal magic or special power of leadership.

compatriot A countryman, colleague, or friend.

contentious Characterized by quarreling or disagreements.

criterion A standard by which something is judged or based.

derisively In a scornful manner.

disheveled Disordered; in disarray.

effigy A crude image or figure representing a hated person.

effusive Excessively demonstrative.

enmity Hostility or ill will.

envoy A person sent as a representative of a government to deal with another government.

faction A party or group, most often only concentrated on their own interests.

firebrand Something that agitates or causes unrest.

fractious Tending to be troublesome.

gaunt Excessively thin, especially if as the result of suffering or a severe personality.

harangue To lecture.

hewer One who fells by blows of an ax; a logger.

Huguenot A French Protestant.

illicit Unlawful.

impartiality Equal treatment.

indefatigable Tireless.

indispensable Absolutely necessary or essential.

lackey A footman or servant; someone who runs errands for someone else.

lionize To treat as someone of great importance.

monarchy Government by a king or queen.

onerous Troublesome.

oxymoron A figure of speech or phrase combining contra-dictory words.

partisan A firm believer in a certain party, group, or faction, often with prejudice or blind allegiance.

polymath One who is expert, skilled, or knowledgeable in a number of different fields or subject matters.

pompous Self-important; arrogant.

precocious Exhibiting adult or mature qualities at an early age.

revered Honored or adored.

scintillating Sparkling, exciting, or stimulating.

sovereign Independent; autonomous.

stringent Severe.

supercargo The officer on a merchant ship responsible for the commercial concerns of the voyage.

vendetta A usually prolonged series of retaliatory or hostile acts in response to the same type of hostility.

voluble Talkative.

wily Crafty; sly.

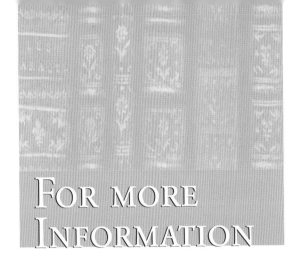

FOR MORE INFORMATION

Friends of John Jay Homestead
P. O. Box 148
Katonah, NY 10536
Phone: (914) 232-8119
Email: friends@johnjayhomestead.org

WEB SITES

Due to the changing nature of Internet links, the Rosen Publishing Group, Inc. has developed an online list of Web sites related to the subject of this book. This site is updated regularly. Please use this link to access the list:

http://www.rosenlinks.com/lat/joja

FOR FURTHER READING

Bailyn, Barnard, ed. *The Debate on the Constitution*. New York, NY: Library of America, 1993.

Bowen, Catherine Drinker. *Miracle at Philadelphia: The Story of the Constitutional Convention*. Boston, MA: Back Bay, 1986.

Collier, Christopher. *Building a New Nation: The Federalist Era, 1789–1801*. New York, NY: Benchmark, 1998.

Collier, Christopher, and John Lincoln Collier. *The American Revolution: 1763–1783*. New York, NY: Benchmark, 1999.

Feinberg, Barbara. *The Articles of Confederation*. New York, NY: 21st Century, 2002.

Jaffe, Steven. *Who Were the Founding Fathers? Two Hundred Years of Reinventing American History*. New York, NY: Henry Holt, 1996.

Nardo, Don. *The Creation of the U.S. Constitution*. Westport, CT: Greenhaven, 2004.

Powell, Phelan. *John Jay: First Chief Justice of the Supreme Court*. Broomall, PA: Chelsea House, 2000.

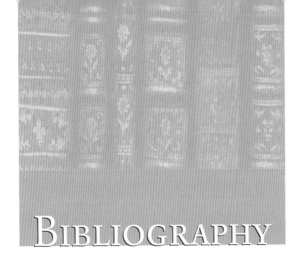

BIBLIOGRAPHY

Bailyn, Bernard, ed. *The Debate on the Constitution.* New York, NY: Library of America, 1993.

Bailyn, Bernard. *The Ideological Origins of the American Revolution.* Cambridge, MA: Harvard, 1980.

Chernow, Ron. *Alexander Hamilton.* New York, NY: Penguin, 2005.

Elkins, Stanley, and Eric McKitrick. *The Age of Federalism: The Early American Republic, 1788–1800.* New York, NY: Oxford, 1993.

Foner, Eric. *Tom Paine and Revolutionary America.* New York, NY: Oxford, 2005.

Freeman, Douglas Southall. *Washington.* New York, NY: Simon & Schuster, 1995.

Ketcham, Ralph, ed. *The Anti-Federalist Papers and the Constitutional Convention Debates.* New York, NY: Signet, 2003.

McCullough, David. *John Adams.* New York, NY: Simon & Schuster, 2001.

Peterson, Merrill. *Thomas Jefferson and the New Nation.* New York, NY: Oxford, 1970.

Rosenfeld, Richard N. *American Aurora*. New York, NY: St. Martin's, 1997.

Scigliano, Robert, ed. *The Federalist: A Commentary on the Constitution of the United States*. New York, NY: Random House, 2000.

Stahr, Walter. *John Jay*. New York, NY: Hambledon and London, 2005.

Taylor, Alan. *American Colonies: The Settling of North America*. New York, NY: Penguin, 2001.

Van Doren, Carl. *Benjamin Franklin*. New York, NY: Penguin, 1991.

Wood, Gordon S. *The Creation of the American Republic, 1776–1787*. New York, NY: Norton, 1972.

Wood, Gordon S. *The Radicalism of the American Revolution*. New York, NY: Random House, 1993.

INDEX

A

Adams, John, 8, 9, 10, 11, 13, 14, 15, 18, 51, 64, 65, 67, 68, 73, 76, 85, 89, 91, 93, 94, 98
on John Jay, 69–70
Adams, Samuel, 50, 61, 76
"Address to the People of Great Britain, The," 53–54
"Address to the People of the State of New York," 84
American Revolution/ Revolutionary War, 12, 13, 26, 55, 58, 62, 67, 89, 91–93, 94, 95, 96
anti-Federalists, 79, 84, 93–94
Articles of Confederation, 73, 75–76, 84

B

Boston Massacre, 46
Boston Tea Party, 49, 53

C

colonies, American
France and, 41, 64, 65, 67
Great Britain and, 10–11, 12, 22, 41–50, 53–54, 57, 64, 65, 91–92
Netherlands/Holland and, 21–22, 25, 47, 48
Spain and, 42, 63–64
Committees of Correspondence, 46
Comte de Vergennes, 64
Constitution, U.S., 9, 13, 15, 78, 79, 81, 84–85, 86, 89, 92–94
Constitutional Convention, 10, 75–78, 79
Continental army, 55, 58, 62, 64
Continental Congress, 8, 10, 55–56, 57, 61–63, 64, 71, 84
First, 49–50
Cooper, James Fenimore, 51, 60

D

Declaration of Independence, 9, 57, 58

F

Federalist, The, 8, 81–85
Federalists, 78–79, 93, 94, 96

Founding Fathers, 6, 8, 9, 12–15,
   18, 78
Franklin, Benjamin, 8, 9, 10, 11, 13,
   14, 15, 18, 19, 64, 65–67, 68, 76,
   84, 91, 96
   on John Adams, 67–68
Fraunces Tavern, 40
French and Indian War, 41
French Revolution, 89, 91, 93

G

George III, King, 49, 61
Grotius, Hugo, 29

H

Hamilton, Alexander, 8, 9, 10, 11,
   14, 15, 18, 73, 75, 76, 79, 82, 83,
   86, 91, 93, 96, 97–98
Hancock, John, 76
Henry, Patrick, 11, 50, 51, 76
Huguenots, 23, 27

I

Intolerable Acts, 49

J

Jay, Auguste (grandfather), 23, 24, 25
Jay, James (brother), 26, 27
Jay, John
   as chief justice, 8, 10, 16, 58,
      86–88, 98
   characteristics of, 30–33
   early life of, 18, 25–26
   education of, 26–29, 30, 32
   family of, 23–25, 26, 32

   as "forgotten" Founding Father,
      6–12
   in France, 64
   on government, 73–75
   on Great Britain, 50–51, 53–54, 57,
      61, 95
   law and, 33, 36–40, 49
   marriage of, 41
   personality of, 12, 15–16, 26, 27,
      29, 30, 36, 38, 61, 69–70
   religion and, 19, 32
Jay, Mary (mother), 25
Jay, Peter (father), 23, 25, 26, 30, 32, 38
Jay Treaty, 11, 95–96, 97, 98
Jay, William (son), 27–28
Jefferson, Thomas, 8, 9, 10, 11, 12,
   14, 15, 18, 19, 53, 57, 73, 75, 76,
   86, 90, 91

K

Kissam, Benjamin, 36, 37–38, 50
Knox, Henry, 86

L

law, study of, 33, 34–36
Lee, Richard Henry, 50, 51, 53, 73, 76
Lexington and Concord, battles at, 55
Livingston, Robert, 30, 38–39, 40,
   50, 53, 67
Livingston, Sarah, 40–41, 63, 98

M

Madison, James, 8, 9, 10, 14, 18, 73,
   75, 76, 79, 81, 82, 83
Morris, Gouverneur, 61

N

New York (New Amsterdam), history
of, 19–22

P

Paine, Thomas, 90, 91
Philipse, Frederick, 24–25
Provincial Congress of New York,
57–58

S

Saratoga, Battle of, 64
Seven Years' War, 41, 42
slaves/slavery, 25, 26
Sons of Liberty, 46, 49
Spy, The, 60
Stahr, Walter, 84

Stamp Act, 42–45, 46, 50
Stuyvesant, Peter, 22
Supreme Court, U.S., 8, 10, 16,
86–88, 98

T

Tea Act, 48
Townshend Acts, 45, 47, 50
Treaty of Paris, 65, 73

W

Washington, George, 6, 9, 10, 11, 13,
14–15, 18, 19, 55, 58, 61, 62, 64,
69–70, 73, 75, 76, 78, 81, 84, 86,
88, 91, 93, 94, 96, 97, 98

Y

Yorktown, Battle of, 64

About the Author

Casey White grew up virtually in the shadow of the John Jay estate in Katonah, New York, and attended John Jay High School there, which she credits with inspiring her lifelong interest in this now often forgotten figure in American history. She has taught American history for many years, with a special emphasis, in her own studies, on the Federalist period.

Photo Credits

Cover portrait, pp. 1, 87 © Francis G. Mayer/Corbis; cover (background), pp. 7, 20–21, 23 © New York Historical Society, New York, USA/ Bridgeman Art Library; pp. 9, 15 National Portrait Gallery, Smithsonian Institution/Art Resource, NY; pp. 10, 74–75 Architect of the Capitol; pp. 14, 15, 16, 59, 82, 83 Independence National Historical Park; p. 13 The White House Collection (White House Historical Association); pp. 19, 39 Library of Congress Geography and Map Division; pp. 24, 27, 37, 40 Courtesy of John Jay Homestead State Historic Site, New York State Office of Parks, Recreation and Historic Preservation; p. 31 Erich Lessing/Art Resource, NY; p. 35 New York Public Library/Art Resource, NY; pp. 36, 60, 72 Library of Congress Prints and Photographs Division; p. 43, 95 © North Wind Picture Archives; p. 44 © Time-Life Pictures/ Getty Images; pp. 47, 48, 56–57 © Getty Images; p. 51 The Art Archive; p. 52 © Atwater Kent Museum of Philadelphia, courtesy of Historical Society of Pennsylvania Collection/Bridgeman Art Library; p. 63 © Gianni Dagli Orti/Corbis; p. 66 State Department Art Collection; pp. 69, 77; NARA; p. 80 New-York Historical Society; p. 90 Giraudon/ Art Resource, NY; p. 92 National Portrait Gallery, London; p. 95 The Granger Collection; p. 97 © Lee Snider/Photo Images/Corbis.

Designer: Gene Mollica; **Editor:** Leigh Ann Cobb
Photo Researcher: Marty Levick